FAMILIAR VOICE

FAMILIAR VOICE

FROM RADIO BROADCASTER TO BIBLE EXPOSITOR
"THE DAVE THOMPSON STORY"

DAVE THOMPSON

Thompson Theological Publishers
Kalamazoo, Michigan

Familiar Voice: From Radio Broadcaster to Bible Expositor—
The Dave Thompson Story
© 2013 by David Thompson.

All rights reserved. Published by Thompson Theological
Publishers, PO Box 545, Schoolcraft, Michigan 49087.

Cover design: Billie Atkinson
Interior design: Nick Richardson

ISBN 978-0-9891481-0-8

Printed in the United States of America

FOREWORD

FOR MANY YEARS, I have been telling Dave that he needs to write his very unusual story of life and ministry. In my 93 plus years, I have not known of a story quite like this one. Dave's testimony is a very unique demonstration of God's sovereign grace and power in being able to completely transform a life and a mind. It is like reading a contemporary account of the combined testimonies of Augustine and C. I. Scofield.

When David first came into my doctrine class, he looked just like any other student, but by the time he was ready to graduate, it was clear to me that he was not an average student. He has one of the best and quickest minds that I have run across in all my years of teaching. His ability to grasp, systematize and unravel Scripture is very unique. I have told him on many occasions that "God has uniquely gifted him and raised him up for this time in history." If I were back heading up any theological school, he would be the one teacher I would want.

When I went to Dallas Seminary in 1939 and began learning from Lewis Sperry Chafer, I had no idea as to what I was getting into. But by the time I graduated in 1942, I knew the importance of God's Word and God's doctrines and Dave is a link to this legacy.

I highly recommend this story to you. It is like no other you will ever read. What God has done in David's life is truly amazing, but it is no more amazing than what He is capable of doing in any person's life who will turn that life over to Jesus Christ.

JOHN L. MILES
August 2009

(John Miles went home to be with the Lord on November 3, 2009, just three months after writing this Foreword.)

PREFACE

I DON'T ACTUALLY LIKE my testimony. I like stories of young people who come to faith in Jesus Christ early in life and grow up loving the Lord Jesus Christ and the Word of God and then prayerfully seek to do God's will with their lives.

I love to see young men and women in the church who fall in love with the Lord and then watch them grow and develop and desire to be trained so they may serve God in some ministry to which He calls them.

My story is not like that at all. As I said, I don't actually like my testimony, but it is what it is and it is contained in this book for you to read.

I have asked myself why write it? I am now nearing my mid 60's so why go back in time some 35—40 years and tell this story now? I have come up with four reasons:

1. This is an amazing story of God's sovereignty. In the late 70's I left Kalamazoo, Michigan having been a goofball on three radio stations. Now I am back in Kalamazoo teaching the Bible systematically on six radio stations in Michigan and 24 around the nation.

2. This story is about God's great Sovereign ability to completely transform a life and one's goals in life.

3. This story does give hope to any person regardless of their sin or situation in that if they will turn their life over to Jesus Christ, the remaining years of their life can truly be an amazing and a fulfilling adventure.
4. This is a story that magnifies the grace of God, for what He has done with me is certainly not something I deserve or merit.

I want to thank several key people who have truly been part of this journey—my wife Mary who has lived this story; my brother Tim who pointed me in the right theological direction; my former boss Bob Kregel who was an amazing employer and who provided the means for me to go to school and to my dear friend and mentor John Miles who became to me every bit of what Lewis Sperry Chafer was to him.

If God can use this story in any way to help someone, then to Him be all the glory.

DAVID E. THOMPSON, 2012

INTRODUCTION

JUST RECENTLY WE WERE interviewing some people for membership at Texas Corners Bible Church. The people were giving testimony of how they came to faith in Jesus Christ and ultimately how they came to Texas Corners Bible Church.

In the course of their testimony, the husband said, "I used to listen to you years ago on the radio and you used to make me mad." Then he said, "Years later I heard the same voice, but now it was confronting me with the truth of God's Word and that made me mad."

He said "I told my wife that we were going to go to this church one time to hear what you had to say." He said when he came to our church, he discovered that we were very serious about the Bible and as the Bible was systematically being taught, he kept sensing "this is the truth and this is right." One Sunday morning he trusted Jesus Christ as Savior and now he and his wife are part of our church.

Today, I am a very serious Bible expositor. What I mean by this is that I systematically teach straight through books of the Bible. I am so serious about this that I am like John Calvin in the sense that I do not like to have to do special Christmas or Easter messages and would much rather stay right in the book I am expounding.

Through this philosophy I have seen God do some amazing things. I have seen many people come to faith in Jesus Christ and fall in love with the Word of God. I have had the privilege of doing Bible lectures on various books of the Bible at various Bible institutes. I have had the privilege of teaching books of the Bible to pastors in South America. We have put our Bible book expositions on the Internet and thousands of people have downloaded them all over the world. We are on six radio stations in the Kalamazoo, Grand Rapids, Holland and Battle Creek areas plus on 24 other stations all across the United States. We have seen our church grow to the point we need to have multiple services on Sunday.

Many of the people who come to our church say they remember me from my days in radio in the 70's. This is the story of how this all happened.

On June 10, 1976,
in the peak of a very successful
radio career in Kalamazoo, Michigan,
Dave Thompson made a decision
that would change him forever.
This is his story.

CHAPTER ONE

"IF YOU DON'T LIKE ME, I don't like you" were the words that always ended my radio show and June 10, 1976 was no different in that respect. I flipped a microphone switch, said those words, started a record, walked out of the radio station, climbed on my 750 Honda and headed for home.

Mary and me shortly before June 10, 1976.

Me working the afternoon drive.

As I rode down I-94, with the warm Michigan wind blowing in my face, I was thinking about the fact that I had just completed 30 days of a brand new radio contract at WYYY. For five plus years I had worked at WKMI radio. I enjoyed that radio station and the people with whom I worked. I always appreciated the management and, even though I was often in hot water for things I did and said, they continually stood by me and even paid an attorney in Washington to defend my radio antics. David Steere, former owner of Steere Broadcasting Corporation, once told me it cost him $600 every time he had to call his attorney in Washington to get me out of trouble with the FCC.

Most of my years at WKMI, were spent as their afternoon drive-time jock, working from 3 to 7. But our relationship took a negative turn, when the station wanted to put me under contract and we could not agree on one simple subject—money. This was the reason we parted ways and the reason I ended up at WYYY. They gave me the contract I wanted.

In the Kalamazoo radio market, most media people are not typically under a contract. However, because of my marketability, which included a bizarre and obnoxious reputation and some unusually high ratings, a contract would keep me from going to another radio station or market and it also would give me the security I thought I needed.

When I drove my motorcycle into my driveway that summer afternoon, there was absolutely no way anyone could possibly predict in less than four hours I would be on my knees in my living room inviting Jesus Christ into my life to be my Savior. When I climbed off that Honda, that June 10 afternoon, God was the farthest thing from my mind.

If You Don't Like Him, He Won't Like You

WKMI disc jockey Dave Thompson makes a point of being "insane, sarcastic and funny." But actually, it is mostly an act.

Dave Thompson does his thing for four hours a day at the WKMI radio studios.

CHAPTER TWO

I GRADUATED FROM Otsego High School in Otsego, Michigan in 1968. I wasn't a great student, I wasn't a great athlete, although I played varsity sports and I wasn't a great musician, although I participated in the band. I wasn't great at anything. One teacher once said "you don't apply yourself to being good at anything." She was right, I didn't. I liked school and had fun and wasn't too serious about learning or forming future goals or plans. In fact, one counselor told me, "college wasn't something I would probably want to pursue."

After graduation, I went to Kalamazoo Valley Community College for a semester. One course seemed to interest me—Broadcasting 101. I went to Western Michigan University for a while, but collegiate life didn't seem to connect with me so I left. I was drifting from one idea and job to another with no real focus or purpose. In 1969, however, I got interested in radio and inquired as to what license was required. I was told that one needed to have a third class license with broadcast endorsement. I asked where such a license could be obtained and I was told from the FCC in Detroit. So I sent for material, studied for an exam and then my mother and I drove to Detroit to take the test, which I passed.

My first radio job was at a radio station in Otsego—a small 1000 watt station—WAOP. The format was country music and I began by typing the programming logs and running taped and live programs on weekends. It wasn't long before an air shift came available and I took it. I learned how to write and record commercials, do live remote broadcasts, run control boards and even start and restart transmitters. I learned how to do interviews and spin records. Although the job didn't pay much, it was giving me an education which, ultimately for me at the time, was worth more than anything one could learn in a classroom.

CHAPTER THREE

I HAD THE PRIVILEGE OF spending time with several big time, big name entertainers and movie stars along the way. Radio is in the entertainment business and you get to rub shoulders with those in that business. At the peak of my radio popularity, doors opened for me to meet them and have them on my radio show. The list of people who did my radio show or who I emceed programs with in the 70's is quite impressive: Doobie Brothers, Helen Reddy, Gary Wright, Mac Davis, Tony Orlando, Dottie West, Farron Young, Ernest Tubbs, Charlie Daniels, Bobbie Vinton, Alice Cooper, Lillie Tomlin and Bob Hope. Some of them gave me their personal home phone numbers so I could reach them whenever I wanted.

Believe it or not, the two most down to earth entertainers I ever had on my radio show were Alice Cooper and Charlie Daniels. Talk about extreme forms of entertainment. Charlie Daniels is a big man with a big heart and a big hat. He is amazingly talented - especially with a fiddle in his hands. He came out to our radio station one afternoon wearing his big Stetson and sat in on my show, taking phone calls for about two hours with a cab running the entire time at his own expense. He was as common a man and as nice a man as you would ever meet. He liked people and he enjoyed talking to his fans in the Kalamazoo area.

Alice Cooper, when off stage, was a mild mannered, down to earth, truly nice guy. On stage he was a psychological nightmare. But off stage, he was as common a man as there was. In fact, I asked Mr.

Cooper on air why he did such weird things on stage and he never batted an eye in his answer—"because people pay to see it and I make a lot of money"(My paraphrase of his answer).

I liked Alice Cooper. He was real, strange, but real. No phony pretenses. I read some place that he was a preacher's son and I have often wished our paths could cross again.

Helen Reddy was an interesting interview. Her song "I Am Woman" was at the top of the charts and it was reported that she was in a hospital having a baby. I decided to see if I could track her down in the hospital and ask her, on air, about how she connected the concept of her song "I Am Woman, hear me roar" with the reality that she was now a mother, listening to a baby roar. I knew her real last name so I called the hospital and asked to be connected to her room.

Helen was in a hospital in Los Angeles and when I called the hospital, it just so happened that the nurse who answered the phone was originally from Benton Harbor, Michigan. She knew of our radio station so she put the call through to Helen's room.

When Helen answered the phone, she sounded as if she had just had a baby—somewhat groggy. When I asked her how she could justify having a baby—which demanded having some connection with a man—with her song thesis which said she was woman who could do anything she wanted on her own, she responded by saying "Having a baby was what she wanted to do." Actually it was a good answer and I am surprised she didn't slam the phone down. I never knew what happened to that nurse from Benton Harbor, but I have always thought fondly of the risk she took by putting my call through.

Bobby Vinton was a nice down to earth, personable man. Tony Orlando was also a very kind man with an on and off air persona which most performers have.

Famous people have a public and private side to them and rarely do people get to actually see their private side. That side isn't too exciting or fun to be around.

Being an entertainer is not easy. It is a lot of pressure. Most have a tremendous desire to be accepted by people and most devote their entire careers to that objective. Believe me; being famous is not all as glamorous as people seem to think. It is true you have some remuneration, perks and your share of groupies, but it also becomes a very lonely existence.

An actor or actress or entertainer, for example spends his or her entire life playing a part or acting a part. In other words, the entire existence is one of pretending to be something you actually aren't. The problem is, people who invest their whole lives acting out a part, often have difficulty becoming the real person they should be or would like to be. In fact, some are afraid to show who they really are for fear they will lose some of the fame they have worked to achieve.

CHAPTER FOUR

To succeed in the entertainment world, you pretty much have to put yourself and your career above everything and everyone. You must have your own agenda. You actually become your own idol. Your goals and ambitions take priority over any other relationship and therefore, any relationship with anyone is destined to fail. Such was true in my life.

Billboard advertising featuring myself and long-time friend, Jim Higgs.

Llewellyn Confronts Dave Thompson Underdogs Win,

The WKMI Underdogs won their fourth consecutive game Wednesday night, beating the Plainwell faculty 60-41.

Thomson, controversial DJ for WKMI, and Ole' Llewellen, Spanish teacher, had been verbally abusing each other for weeks. Llewellen said she would "stuff the basketball down his throat." Thomson announced on the radio if she tried such action she would leave the game

the game did not hinge on the score but on the expected confrontation between Dave Thomson and Mrs. Llewellen.

is."

It was shortly after halftime when Llewellen decided it was time for action. Thomson, dribbling coolly down the court, spotted the oncoming Llewellen. Llewellen, not wishing to draw a foul, vainly went for the ball. Thomson engaged in frustrating fancy dribbling, between his legs and around his back. Just as Thomson was beginning to enjoy himself, the referee called a jump ball.

Llewellen, although not completely filling her threat, had succeeded in stopping Dave Thomson. Dave Thomson succeeded in proving his point also, showing he is a good sport and a great humorist too.

For the sake of not embarrassing specific people, I will talk in generalities here, but the truth is I was willing to walk away from family, friends and a relationship for the sake of an entertainment career. It is a high price that most are willing to pay when chasing after the fleeting vain shadow called notoriety.

For me, the radio career came first. It was all about me, my goals, my pursuits, my pleasure, my fame, my happiness. If someone got hurt along the way, that was too bad. If they didn't fit in with my pursuits, they got left behind.

If my wife was lonely and crying at home while I was surrounded by beautiful models, actresses or Playboy bunnies who were on my show, that was tough for her. I was working to achieve something for me. If I needed to be out late in a nightclub, I was.

I recall one occasion when I had made a hurtful remark about a local television personality and his wife called me off-air to appeal to me because she felt my remarks were hurtful to her husband and could be hurtful to her children as they went to school and were faced with the ridicule of their school peers. I basically laughed at the whole thing even though what I had said could have brought some hurt to a family, I thought it was funny and it should be funny for them.

That was the frame of mind I had in my world of radio. That was my egotistical drive and passion. Today, I am deeply grieved by these things and take full responsibility for all the wrong I did. If I could turn back the clock and change things I would, but no one can.

CHAPTER FIVE

HAVING JUST SIGNED A new one year radio contract which guaranteed me everything I wanted, one would think I would have been totally happy. I was, at times, the toast of the town. I could go into many restaurants and nightclubs and my open tab would be covered. I was in demand for personal appearances and public events. I did enjoy being connected to many charity events from March of Dimes

We drew big crowds to various things. Here I was doing a fundraiser for March of Dimes.

to Muscular Dystrophy campaigns. One would think this life would be glamorous and happy and fun. I suppose for a while, it seemed to be that way, but in the end it wasn't. Something was missing and lacking. Some part to my life's puzzle just didn't seem to fit.

As I look back on things prior to June 10, 1976, there were three entertainment episodes that started causing me to think about my life's path. I had the privilege of introducing Bob Hope at Wings Stadium one night and we were standing back stage prior to me going out to introduce him. I looked him in the eyes and asked

"Mr. Hope, why do you go night after night to city after city when you have all the money and fame you could possibly want?" I will never forget his answer. He said "I live for the applause." He loved to make people laugh and when they cheered and applauded him, he was totally in his glory zone. I remember after introducing him of standing off stage watching him work and thinking is that my life's goal? Is that what life is all about? Am I after a career that ends with me living for applause of people? Although I couldn't put my finger on the pulse of what was troubling me, something was.

The second episode occurred when I was asked to introduce a very famous band, again at Wings Stadium. I will not name the band, but I will tell the story. I was standing back stage between acts, waiting to introduce the main group when a medical team member came to me and asked if I would go out and make a announcement "would the parents or guardian of ___ please report to a specific gate." It seems that a girl had taken too many drugs and the medical team felt they needed to get her to a hospital and they wanted authorization to take her there. As I started toward the front of the stage to make the announcement, the band's stage manager asked me where I was heading and I told him. He informed me I was not going to make that announcement because it was too negative. I informed him I was going to make the announcement or the girl could die and he said "let her die." To make a long story short, I took a wireless stadium microphone out and made the announcement and the girl ended up to be okay. But this episode started me thinking—"What kind of world am I in?" "Am I out to become like these people?"

A third episode occurred as I was preparing again to introduce a famous band. I don't know about these days but, back in the 70's, record companies wanted their contracted bands introduced a certain way with very specific wording. So I would have to meet with these guys to memorize exactly how they wanted their bands introduced. I was walking in a tunnel with the band after they got out of their limousine and there was a gap of approximately 20 to 30 feet that the tunnel did not cover which allowed people to look down and actually see the band walking in to their dressing room. One lady, who I am sure paid good money for her seat - which was a lousy seat - saw the band come in and yelled "Hi." The lead singer looked up and shouted obscenities at this woman who had just said hello. Again, I began to wonder, what kind of people are these entertainment people?

These three episodes stirred my mind in the mid-70's and I continually wondered if I were after the same goals they were. If my plan was to become like these people, would I end up like them? I was haunted by this. I could not shake the nagging questions about my goals and objectives in life.

CHAPTER SIX

JUNE 10, 1976 WAS THE greatest life transforming day of my life. What happened on that day is absolutely amazing and in almost a Pauline fashion, I was stopped dead in my tracks at age 26.

The radio show under my new contract went from 2:00PM— 6:00PM. As I pulled into my driveway after the show, I had one thought in mind—go down in the basement and smoke a joint. I went down and started looking in some boxes where I thought it was and all of a sudden there, in the bottom of a box, all covered with dust was a Bible.

At the time I picked up this Bible, I did not know if God even existed. Even though as a boy I had gone to Sunday School and church, I had not really personally embraced what that church had to offer.

I recall taking that Bible out onto our patio and sitting down on a lawn chair and looking up into the sky, wondering if there really was a God. I would say this all started about 7:00PM. I did not know any book of the Bible, so I opened up to the index and picked a book to read. The first was Titus. I don't have any idea to this day why I selected this book. Titus is a pastoral book, basically written to give instruction to leadership. I have always thought it is possible that God was showing me from this initial moment where He was going to send me—to pastoral leadership.

As I finished reading Titus, it was turning dark. So I went inside to our living room and sat down and went back to the index and this

YYY Thompson?

Kalamazoo's top D.J. increases amplitude

BY BILL ROBINSON
Staff Writer

Kalamazoo's highest paid disc jockey, Dave Thompson, begins his first day with WYYY today.

FOR FIVE YEARS Thompson worked for WKMI, a major crosstown competitor, and was recognized as the top disc jockey in Kalamazoo.

At a news conference Wednesday, Thompson signed what he thought was the first contract in Kalamazoo broadcasting. Although he and WYYY owner and operator Emil J. (Bud) Popke refused to say how much money Thompson would be paid, it was understood he will be getting a big raise over his WKMI salary.

Besides Thompson and other WYYY employees, Thompson's lawyer, James Brignall, also came to the news conference. Thompson said Brignall helped with the legal aspects of the contract.

Herald Photo by PAUL BUSHOUSE

Kalamazoo's top disc jockey Dave Thompson signs new contract with Bud Popke of station WYYY. Thompson—in a surprise move—last week left WKMI, where he had been employed the last five years.

Notice the date of this event—May 10, 1976. God saved me June 10, 1976.

time I picked John the fourth book of the New Testament. I have tried to remember what was going on in my mind as I was reading these books and the only clear thing I can recall is that I concluded that "God had a plan for my life and this entire plan hinged on having Jesus Christ in my life as my personal Savior."

I do not specifically remember how long it took me to read all 21 chapters in John's Gospel, but it was very late. I do remember exactly what happened as I finished reading it. I literally got down on my knees in my living room and bowed my head and said something like this—"God I know I am a sinner and I also know that I need Jesus Christ in my life to give me meaning so I am turning my life over to you and I ask Christ to be my personal Savior. Here is my life. Take it and use it." Those were basically my prayer words that night.

In the aftermath of making this prayer, something powerful happened. I certainly did not know theology or doctrine at this point, but I certainly did know something powerful had just happened. One of the things that happened is that I had an overwhelming sense of how much of a sinner I was. I simply started to cry. Here I was, on my knees in my living room, and I am overwhelmed with how much of a sinner I was and I was weeping about it. As I now know, the convicting work of the Holy Spirit was in full force. There was also a sense in which a huge weight had just been lifted off my shoulders. I felt good, I felt free, I felt fulfilled. I am not a real mystical guy, but there was something very mystical about what was happening that night.

It must have been 2:00AM or 3:00AM when I crawled into bed. Even though I didn't understand all the theological ramifications of what had just happened, I knew something about me was very different.

CHAPTER SEVEN

THE NEXT MORNING I got up and something was again drawing me to pick up the Bible.

I was in the living room and again was reading the Bible. My wife, Mary, looked in and asked what I was doing and said, "I am reading the Bible because last night I invited Jesus Christ into my life." She looked at me as if I were nuts.

My wife had to put up with a lot being married to me because I was a hard core sinner and did not make any false pretenses about it. I lived life as an Augustine, prior to his conversion.

I was a hedonistic heathen so when my then Catholic wife saw me with a Bible in my hands, she thought I had lost my mind.

I remember thinking I ought to go to a Christian book store and see if I could find a book that would help me understand the Bible better. Even though today I have thousands of books in my library, I can still remember the first two I bought—*Matthew Henry's Commentary on the Whole Bible* and Warren Wiersbe's little commentary on Ephesians entitled *Be Rich*. In fact, I still have the amount I paid for that little book from the Zondervan store, $1.95. Years later I would have the privilege of meeting Dr. Wiersbe (he signed my Bible with the reference Psalm 16:11) and it actually would be something he wrote to me in a personal letter that God would use to change my life. I purchased his little commentary and devoured it, having no idea what God ultimately had in store for me.

That day I had a radio show to do, but I didn't feel the same as I went to the station. I didn't know all what had happened, but I found myself in the next days not wanting to do anything off color or say things that could hurt people. In fact, I didn't want to play certain songs because of what they seemed to suggest. Keep in mind, to this point, I am not in a church and have not talked to any minister. This was purely God at work in me.

When people want to quibble about the sovereignty of God or the election of God, they are

talking to the wrong guy when they talk to me. Without any other explanation other than God's sovereignty, God saved me and started a transforming work that still is operative to this very day.

CHAPTER EIGHT

THIRTY DAYS AFTER TRUSTING Christ as Savior, now sixty days into a new radio contract, my personality had dramatically changed. I wasn't the same person anymore. I knew it and so did the management of the radio station for which I worked.

I was summoned to a meeting to discuss these changes and, as I recall, the meeting included the Radio Station Owner, General Manager, Sales Manager and Program Director.

Actually, I liked all of these guys and they seemed to like me so this was not going to be an easy meeting for either of us.

When I went into the office and sat down, the essence of what happened was this.

The management said "We have in good faith negotiated a contract with you for a year and something has changed and things seem to be different and we just want to know what is going on."

I shared with them that I had trusted Jesus Christ as my Savior and that I was not the same person anymore and would not be doing the same kinds of things I used to do on the radio. I knew that put them in a bind so I said if they wanted to tear up the contract, I would leave quietly and not contest it and we could part ways this very day. To my amazement, they were very gracious and said they would honor the contract to the end and actually when I finally did leave, they were kind enough to offer another contract.

In the next ten months on the air, I had some interesting on air phone conversations. I had people call in and discuss various topics. I called it "Speak Out of Your Head" or "Vibrate Through Your Teeth." It was amazing, but in the final ten months of my contract, there were topics discussed on contemporary radio that you would expect to hear on Christian radio.

For example, I recall one program where the topic was this—"If it is proved that Jesus Christ was raised from the dead then what exactly are the ramifications?" Another topic was "If a remnant of Noah's ark was actually discovered, what would that mean about the Bible?" People were phoning in and we were discussing this on a Top 40, contemporary radio station.

Actually the final ten months of my radio contract were amazing and even though I had another contract offered, I felt God wanted me out of this career, so I declined and left. In my final show, I didn't say "If you don't like me, I don't like you", what I said was something to this effect, "If you didn't like me, I understand that, but I want you to know I did really care about you and so does God."

With that, I gathered my things and left for a journey that would be truly amazing.

CHAPTER NINE

I GOT A JOB IN A paper mill. Some of the jobs were interesting. I enjoyed driving a fork lift and running a beater. I didn't enjoy crawling under rollers and hiking out broken paper and I sure didn't like cleaning the sewers from eleven at night until seven in the morning. But that was the job I got when I left radio.

During this time I learned a lot about work, a lot about people and a lot about real life. That job was good for me because this was the real world where real people work hard to earn a living. There is nothing glamorous about the jobs in the mill, but men supported their families and did their work every day and week.

It was during this time that I began to wonder if this was where God wanted me for the rest of my life? I must admit this was not where I wanted to be for the rest of my life, but I concluded that if this were where God wanted me, I was willing to stay there. I had no idea what God had in store for me, but all I knew is that I wanted to do what He wanted me to do. Someone said "doing the will of God with your life is 99% being willing to do the will of God with your life before you actually know what it is." That was my heart's desire that year in 1977.

From a spiritual perspective I was growing. I was reading my Bible, I was going to church and I was buying and reading books. When I had questions, I would ask my brother, since he was the one who had a theological education. During that year my wife, Mary, came to faith in Jesus Christ and it was just about this time that I began to wonder if there were places where you could go to actually learn things about the Bible.

CHAPTER TEN

WHEN MY BROTHER TIM was about twelve, he had gone to a Christian camp with some friends. Both of us, to this day, are early risers and Tim would get up in the early morning and go for a walk to look for deer. One morning at this camp, he met a man walking and the man asked Tim what he was doing and Tim said, "looking for deer." Tim reciprocated and asked the man what he was doing and the man said "I like to get up early and walk and talk with the Lord." My brother Tim never forgot that man and years later this man would play a vital role in Tim's life and ultimately my life. His name was John Miles. (As a postscript to this story, when John Miles was 92 years old, I asked him if he remembered meeting Tim on that road and he replied that he vividly remembered it and could see it in his mind)

John Miles was President of the Grand Rapids School of the Bible and Music for over 40 years. In fact, I would go so far as to say, 'he was the school.' When he first was asked to by Malcolm Cronk to help form the school in 1946, he was Academic Dean and was responsible to form a curriculum. Since he had studied under Lewis Sperry Chafer at Dallas Seminary, he decided to implement basically that same curriculum he was trained under at Dallas. John Miles had been personally taught and influenced by Lewis Sperry Chafer starting in 1939 and Lewis Sperry Chafer had been personally taught and influenced by the great Bible scholar, C.I. Scofield.

In his own autobiography, John Miles described Dr. Chafer: "He

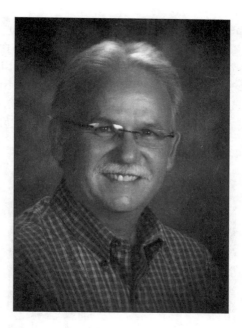

My brother, Tim, who was a big influence on my life. He graduated from
Grand Rapids School of the Bible, Calvin College and Dallas Theological Seminary.
He worked for years ministering to the Jews in St. Louis, then moved north of Atlanta
and co-founded a Bible church.

was a small, slender man, I would guess about five feet tall. There
was always a dignity about him. When he spoke or taught, there was
nothing bombastic or oratorical. However, there was an intensity
and conviction and authority that held me spellbound....I learned a
lot....I became firmly established in salvation by grace. Theology was
taught in the atmosphere of having a spiritual life to go with it. I was
challenged, especially by the life and teaching of Dr. Chafer to a life
of faith."(John Miles, *The Thrill of the Ministry Lessons of Fifty-five
Plus Years*, p.48)

I do not believe it was a chance meeting between my brother Tim
and John Miles because years later Tim would go to this school and

graduate and then go on to Dallas Theological Seminary and it would be my brother Tim who said in 1977, "if you want to truly learn the Bible, there is a great school in Grand Rapids, Michigan and you ought to take a look at it." Little did I know at the time, but John Miles would become the greatest influence of my spiritual life and he would become my dear friend and much more will be said about him later.

John Miles taken by me at my final visit with him at Frontier School of the Bible in LaGrange, Wyoming. Notice his Chafer Systematic Theology numbered 1–7.

CHAPTER ELEVEN

IN THE FALL OF 1977, I took a drive to Grand Rapids, Michigan to look into this school my brother had recommended. I knew nothing about theology or biblical studies. The school was the old Calvin College campus and it was beautiful. I recall walking into the administration building and asking for a catalog.

I took the catalog back out to my car and began to look through it. What was so odd is that I didn't even understand much of the language of the courses. There were courses with titles such as Hermeneutics, Homiletics, Greek Exegesis. There were terms like Hamartiology, Ecclesiology and Eschatology. The strange thing was as I read this catalogue, there was something stirring in me to want to learn these things. I now know that the stirring was the Holy Spirit, but at that time all I knew is this is where I wanted to go to learn.

There were plenty of courses I could understand. There were various books of the Bible that were required and there was a course on Evangelism and Old and New Testament Survey.

As I glanced through this catalogue, my soul stirred, wanting to learn the Word of God and the Doctrines of God.

CHAPTER TWELVE

I KNEW IF I WERE TO be able to go to this school, I would need a job in Grand Rapids.

So in early 1978, when I would work the 3-11 shift at the paper mill or the 11-7 shift, I would head to Grand Rapids, pick up a paper and go fill out applications for a job. I filled out so many applications that I still remember my hand hurting and the indentation that was in my finger.

One thing that I truly believe is critical to this part of my story: every time I filled out an application I prayed before I went in and I prayed when I turned the application in. I always asked God to give me the job He wanted me to have. When I turned in the application, I would bow my head and pray "God if this is the job for me so I can go to this school to learn your Word, grant me this job.' I left it entirely in God's hands and for a while, it almost appeared as if God would never lead me to the right job.

On one of my trips to Grand Rapids, I was looking through the job opportunities and saw an opening for someone who could write radio and television commercials for WOOD radio. I spotted that and thought for sure, this is it. I immediately drove to the broadcast facility, walked in and said "I am here to apply for the job to write commercials." I was asked, "Have you ever written commercials before?" I immediately responded, "Yes, many times."

They asked me if I would be willing to write a commercial and I said "yes." So they brought me some cold copy and I asked if they wanted a 30 second or 60 second commercial and it seems to me they said 60 second, but my memory is fuzzy on this point. When I was done, I gave them the copy and they looked it over and then gave me an application and said to fill it out, which I did. When I was done, I turned it in and headed for Kalamazoo.

As was my habit, I had prayed before I went in and after I had turned in the application. As soon as I walked into my living room, the phone rang and it was the program director for the radio station. He said "Dave, we would like to talk with you. You have a job and when can you be here to talk." I told him the next day. I was thrilled. My heart soared. I thanked God. This would be a perfect job. I could write commercials for radio and television and go to school and get a theological education.

The next day I drove to Grand Rapids fully expecting this was my job to get me to Grand Rapids. But I was in for a big surprise. When I got to the station, the program director invited me into his office. As I recall, this was the essence of what he said, "Dave, you have a job here, but we don't want you writing commercials, we want you on the air. We know of your reputation in Kalamazoo and we want you to go back on the air." I responded by saying "I want to move here to go to school." He said, "We know that and we will work with you on it. You can go to school and then come in and do your show."

As I sat in his office, I silently prayed and asked God for wisdom in what I should do. On the one hand, I could do a four or five hour radio show and go to school, but on the other hand, this job would put me back into the world I just came out of. This was my dilemma. I looked at Bill and said something to this effect: "Bill, thank you for this wonderful opportunity, but I think I better decline. I just came out of this business and I don't think God wants me back in it right now." We shook hands and I left.

As I drove home to Kalamazoo, I thought, God I hope I made the right decision.

CHAPTER THIRTEEN

WEEKS BEFORE THIS JOB opportunity at WOOD radio came my way, I had filled out a resume for a job at Kregel Publications. I had heard through a friend of my aunt that there may be some opening in the shipping department and so I had gone there and filled out an application.

The very next day, after turning down the radio opportunity, my phone rang and I was informed I could have the job if I wanted it and I immediately took it. Little did I know that this would turn out to be one of the greatest jobs in my life.

My first job at Kregel was in the shipping department. My job was to see that the shelves were stocked with books, fill book orders and ship them. When I first went to work for Kregel, I didn't know a whole lot about their books or what they published, but by the time I left Kregel, I had personally read almost every one of their books.

Louis Kregel initially started peddling books to ministers and when his son, Bob Kregel took over, he turned it into one of the most significant theological book publishers in the world.

He decided to produce classic theological works of the old scholars so serious minded people could still get their hands on their writings.

When I first started packing books, I had no idea as to the influence some of those books had made on the world. For example, I personally shipped out hundreds of books on Romans and Galatians written by Martin Luther with absolutely no idea who Martin Luther

Robert L. Kregel, Founder of Kregel Publications.

was or the Reformation impact he had made. What I did find in-triguing is that one of the first courses I actually took at the Grand Rapids School of the Bible and Music was Galatians and the teacher mentioned Martin Luther. I remember thinking, "hey that is the guy whose books I just shipped."

Bob Kregel had an unbelievable God-given knack for selecting classic theological works. He knew many men in ministry and he told me he would consult with them and get their suggestions. But he always made the final decision. Between Bob and his brother Ken, if there was an old classic theological work anywhere in the world, they knew of it and would often travel overseas to get it.

The reason why I take the time to present this is because, this

Ken Kregel and myself in the Kregel Publications booth at the
1983 Christian Booksellers Association Convention.

became a key part of my education. Bob told me to take any book
I wanted and read it and I did just that. In fact, today I have thou-
sands of books in my library and many of them are from Kregel
Publications.

As I would read these books and as I was going to school, God was
stirring my mind and heart. I was driven to understand the Bible and
any book that could help me do that, I wanted it. I was fortunate to
be working for a publisher that only published good works because
very early on I was reading some of the best books about God that
had ever been published.

Bob Kregel worked with me all the way through school. He
was a gracious and generous man. A few months after working in

shipping, he named me Shipping Manager. I worked for a couple of years in that capacity until he asked me if I would be willing to go to Cincinnati, Ohio to make a book presentation to a group of pastors. He told me to see if I could clear things at school, which I did, and I traveled to Cincinnati to make a twenty minute book presentation. I prayed all the way there and in the end we sold several books and Bob promoted me into sales. He sat up an office for me and after school, I would go to work and call various Bible institutes, Bible colleges, Bible seminaries and Christian book stores all over the country. I would come up with some special, he would approve it and I would get on the phone and sell it. After one year of this, he promoted me to Sales Manager.

I have often thought about how rich an education I received working for Kregel. I met authors, such as Warren Wiersbe, John Walvoord, Chuck Swindoll. I read hundreds of solid books and I worked for a man who loved God and His Word.

I have often thought the best decision God ever led me to make was to turn down a radio job because the job at Kregel was priceless.

CHAPTER FOURTEEN

THE GRAND RAPIDS SCHOOL of the Bible and Music was a theological institute designed to teach one thing, the Bible. That is why I chose that school because that is what I wanted. I wasn't interested in studying business or broadcasting, nor was I interested in studying math or medicine. What I wanted was knowledge of the Bible. There was a driving force in me that wanted to know God's Word. I certainly do not minimize those other disciplines or those who pursue those other areas of study, but I wanted a school that taught the Bible and that was the specific focus of this school. It was a technical school designed for one purpose, the Bible and that is why we moved to Grand Rapids.

As I have said, I am not much of a mystical guy, but there was something sacred about that campus that I sensed the first day I went to a class and I continued to sense it years later when I left Grand Rapids. In fact, there were many times when I would be so overwhelmed by the presence of God on that campus that I would literally bow my head and thank God for the privilege of being in such a wonderful place of learning. I have come to believe that the powerful presence of God was due to one man, Mr. John Miles.

The campus of the Grand Rapids School of the Bible and Music was the old Calvin College on Franklin Street in Grand Rapids, Michigan. The story of how this became the Bible institute is a story of the grace and power of God and it is a story of an amazing answer to a prayer prayed specifically by John Miles. In his own autobiography, John Miles gives his own account of what happened:

> "The downtown campus student body grew to 546, and we recognized that we were at capacity. My home was located in the southeast section of Grand Rapids...about a four mile walk to the downtown location of the school. Frequently I would walk to school early in the morning. About six blocks from my home I would walk past the vacated campus of Calvin College. Calvin had grown to the point that they had to relocate, and they developed a new campus off the East Beltline....As I walked past the old Calvin property, I would pray, "Lord give us this property." Others may have been praying as well, but the request was fresh to me each time I walked or drove past that campus." (John Miles, *The Thrill of the Ministry: Lessons of Fifty-Five Plus Years*, p.104) God answered that prayer and in 1972 the old Calvin College campus became the location for the Grand Rapids School of the Bible and Music.

CHAPTER FIFTEEN

Now that I had my new job in Grand Rapids, we put everything we owned up for sale and sold it and moved to Grand Rapids. Soon after we moved in 1978, I signed up for four courses in the evening school—Christian Ethics, Spiritual Life, Personal Evangelism and Philippians. I would get up and go to work and then after work go to school. Mary stayed home with our son Chris and I would get home and she would have dinner and then I would hit the books. I always asked God to give me wisdom to understand things from His word.

In 1979, one of the required courses was Bible Doctrine and the man who taught it was John Miles. What Lewis Sperry Chafer was to John Miles, John Miles was to me. John Miles had designed a specific freshman-required course which was for the purpose of giving a doctrinal overview of all of the doctrines of the faith. He designed and wrote a thorough doctrinal notebook and workbook which were required for the course. He told me that he basically took all of the theology that he had learned from Dr. Chafer and systematized it for a one year freshman course.

Today, I own and have read and studied most theologies that have been written, but I must say I have never seen any other work in print that is equal to capturing the essence of doctrine as the notes written by John Miles. What is even more amazing about his notes is that he only had a few weeks to compile it and yet they are so thorough that his notes are still used in various Bible institutions to this day.

There was nothing flashy about John Miles. When I first saw him, he was in his early 60's. He had gray hair and seemed to be relatively small in stature and very dignified.

He appeared to me to be a humble and quiet man, which was totally the opposite of any person I had ever met in the entertainment world. He seemed to have a confidence and steadfastness to him and when I was in his presence, I knew this was not some spiritual lightweight of a man.

I vividly remember walking into that first doctrine class and there was this man named John Miles who was about to start a lecture. We had our Bibles, our notebooks, our workbooks and our pens. Roll was taken and prayer was offered and he began his lecture on the importance of doctrine. The moment he opened up his mouth, there was something powerful, gripping and dynamic about what he was teaching. Things he was saying were lighting up my soul and connecting in my mind and heart. I had literally stood on the stages with some of the biggest entertainers in the world and I had been in many church services, but when I listened to this man teach, there was a power and authority I had never experienced before. What I would come to know is that he had an authority that truly did come from knowing God's Word and from years of walking with God. Not one time did he ever try to impress you but when his classes were over, you were always impressed.

Doctrine became my favorite class and this man became my favorite teacher and years later he would become my dear friend. I couldn't wait to get to his class, no matter how tired I may have been from work or no matter what pressures I was facing in life. When each class ended, I couldn't believe it was over and that a 50 minute lecture had gone so fast. This was a man who not only knew doctrine and theology but this was a man who knew the God who inspired it. What this man had is what I wanted and what he was is what I wanted to become.

Very early in my days of theological education, I started asking God to give me the kind of wisdom and knowledge and spirituality that he gave John Miles.

CHAPTER SIXTEEN

GOD HAD BEEN GOOD and I had made it through my first year in school, juggling work and school. In 1979, our second son, Adam, was born so Mary had her hands full at home. She was working odd jobs to help make ends meet and she was caring for the boys and me. Courses at school came to life, and by God's grace I did very well academically. Going to Bible school was never a burden for me, it was always a joy although there were times I would get weary and there were some teachers (I will not name) that made some classes less joyful. Academically, I was now faced with a decision which for me was monumental decision—do I study the Greek language?

The Grand Rapids School of the Bible and Music taught Bible and stressed the English Bible. In fact, every student, regardless of their scholastic emphasis, was a Bible major. But John Miles knew the importance of the original languages, since he himself had studied them and one of the majors that was offered was a major in the Greek language.

This became a big decision for me to make because I was working full time, I had not been a great student in any school and I didn't know much about our own English language, much less some foreign language that was used 2000 years ago. If someone would have asked me in those days to define syntax, I would probably have said, "some fine you pay for sin."

But something was prompting me to sign up for this course, which would eventually become my major. I reasoned that knowing this language would help me know God's written Word better. I recall talking with God about this and my prayer was something like this— "God you inspired your New Testament in Greek and I truly want to know your Word and you know I am ignorant of grammar and yet you have led me every step of the way to this school and I am asking you to lead me to understand the Greek language that is taught at this school." With much fear and trepidation, I signed up for the study of the Greek language.

There were two teachers who taught first year Greek and to this day, I believe God gave me the better of the two. His name was Mr. McIntyre. On the first day of class, he walked into class and said this: "Gentlemen, you are here to learn the Greek language and I am going teach you this from the ground up. I want you to forget everything you know about language because I want you to think as a Greek student. When we talk about a Greek noun, I will define noun. When we talk about a Greek adjective, I will define adjective. You are going to learn Greek as a Greek student, not as an English student."

That teacher will never know what that opening statement did for me, because I thought, "I'll have a chance of learning this stuff." What he didn't know is that I couldn't think like an English student because I didn't know English well enough, so learning to think as a Greek student wouldn't be much of a stretch. Truth is, when you formally study another language, it will make you a better English student, because it will force you to learn much about the English language.

For the next three years, I pursued a study of Greek along with my other studies. I must say that I did have a great instructor for the intermediate and graduate level of Greek study, Mr. William Brew. Bill Brew had also been trained at Dallas Theological Seminary and he was a very proficient professor.

The thing that stands out in my mind about his teaching is that biblical Greek was not just about Greek words and forms or parsing Greek verbs, it was about a grammatical context. He made us grammatically diagram passages in Greek and then defend our diagram either on paper or in class.

I recall that in one of our early Greek exegetical assignments, I worked hours on diagramming and preparing a paper and when I got it back, he said, basically "you did a lot of good work, but next time figure out what the passage is actually talking about, because you missed the whole point." He was right and in pure grace he gave me a good grade, but this was a key turning point in my approach to Scripture. I have always appreciated what he taught me and it has stuck with me all of these years. Little bulbs began to go on in my mind and heart and I began to see the grammatical flow of thought. My passion was to know exactly what a text said and this became a critical tool to help me do this.

When all was said and done, I completed twenty hours of formal study of the Greek Language, including 8 hours of Greek Grammar; 3 hours of Greek Syntax, and 9 hours of Greek Exegesis. God had answered my prayer. By His amazing grace I was able to grasp it and love it.

In fact, I would also go on to formally study the Hebrew language.

When you think about the fact that I trusted Jesus Christ in a radio career in 1976 and then seven years later had completed a thorough study of the Greek Language, it is an amazing testimony to the transforming power of the grace of God.

Some have said that learning came natural for me. This is not true. It took much prayer and it took hard work. I would get home from work or school, eat dinner and hit the books. I would study until I got so tired that I was just staring at words. I would get up very early in the morning and study before school or work and did this for five years. This is the way I learned. I would pray and ask God to help me grasp His Word and then study. That is what God honored.

I have often been asked whether or not a person could be effective in ministry without a formal study of biblical languages and my answer is 'yes'. One could be effective without a formal study of languages if one were a very serious student who would avail himself of proper grammatical tools. H.A. Ironside, the old Bible scholar from Moody Church in Chicago, only had an eighth grade education, but he was a disciplined student, who literally studied himself blind.

I doubt seriously that men who go into ministry who are not serious students of God's Word will ever hear "well done good and faithful servant" especially in view of the fact that Paul told Timothy to study to rightly divide Scripture so that he would not be a workman who would end up ashamed (2 Timothy 2:15). Personally, I think biblical languages are great opportunities for men preparing for ministry to trust God to learn them. If God inspired His Word in a particular language, it stands to reason that He would permit men serious about His Word to grasp the language He inspired at a level that would be helpful in unraveling His Word.

CHAPTER SEVENTEEN

I AM ALWAYS AMAZED by those who go to a theological institution, knowing exactly where they are headed and what God is calling them to do, because I had no clue. In fact, as I have already said, my initial reason for going to school was to learn the Bible, but the more I learned the Bible, the more I wanted to do the will of God with my life, so I prayed about that.

The Grand Rapids School of the Bible and Music was a three year institution. However, they offered two more years of graduate level courses, which for me strung out my formal training to five years. Sometime during my junior year, at one of the chapel services at school, a missionary speaker posed this question: "If God were to call you right now to go to Africa, would you be willing to go and would you be willing to tell God that?"

That question hit me right between the eyes and my first reaction was, I don't want to go to Africa. I don't like the heat and I am not really interested in crawling through jungles with things that can kill you. Beside that, that is David Livingstone's territory and Paul said he was careful not to build on another man's work.

But, the truth is, this question kept nagging me. Would I be willing to go to Africa if that is where God wanted me to go and would I be willing to tell God that? I finally concluded that I would because I knew that if I were right where I was supposed to be by the will of God, I would be happy and fulfilled. There could be no better place than to be where God wanted you to be. I went to God and prayed something like this: "God if you want me in Africa, I am willing to go because I truly do want to do your will with my life."

Having come to this conclusion, I felt it was only fitting to pose the same question to my wife Mary. Mary has been a wonderful wife. Being married to me since 1973 is no easy assignment but she has been at my side through everything. She came to faith in Christ in 1977, and has become a tremendous minister's wife. She will help any person with anything at any time. She is a skilled organizer and is capable of heading large banquets at the drop of a hat. She is a great decorator and all of our churches have taken advantage of that and she is an amazing prayer warrior.

When I got home, I posed exactly the same question to her that had been posed to us in chapel. I said, "Don't answer me now, but think about it and pray about it and I would like to hear your answer." In the end, she said "If God calls you to Africa; I am willing to go for doing God's will would always be the best thing to do."

We were willing to go wherever God wanted, but I must say, I am not too disappointed that Africa would not be where He would send us.

CHAPTER EIGHTEEN

As I started my fifth and final year in school, Bob Kregel named me Sales Manager of Kregel Publications. I juggled my final year's schedule so I could travel on off school days and be in school on class days. It was not uncommon for me to jump on a plane, fly somewhere, rent a car, call on Christian book stores and then fly home so I could be in school. I never wanted to miss any class.

As graduation approached in 1983, I still had no idea what God had in store, but then one day I was summoned to the office of John Miles. He said he would like me to consider teaching some courses the next year on a part time basis. I reminded him that Bob Kregel had made me Sales Manager and I would need to talk this over with him. Mr. Miles said, "You talk it over with Bob (John Miles knew Bob Kregel and Bob Kregel knew John Miles and both highly respected each other) because I want you to teach and we'll work around your schedule and perhaps you can do both."

By this time, I had developed a close friendship with John Miles. He was like no other man I had ever met. He had an amazing confidence in God and a profound grasp of the grace of God. This was not only evidenced in the classroom, but in the way he associated with stumble bumbs like me. I still recall being in his office on many occasions and we would pray about various things. More than once he would say "Let's pray about this right now" and we would.

God had truly blessed my studies and by the time I got to my final

John Miles shaking my hand at graduation.

year, which for me was year five, my reputation was that of a very serious student of Scripture. By God's amazing grace He had permitted me to do very well academically. I am sure that this played into Mr. Miles decision a little, but more than anything it was about a dear man of God demonstrating the pure grace of God to an unworthy vessel. I was being asked to teach at a theological institution and I was humbled and honored.

I left the office of John Miles that day and got in my car and thanked God and I began to cry. I sat there and thought what marvelous things God had just done. In 1976, I was a miserable wretch of a sinner in radio going nowhere in life and now, seven years later, I was being asked to teach the Bible. I never believed for one instant that

I had deserved any of this, but this is what God did do and in 1984, I was a part-time faculty member and Bible teacher at a theological institution in Grand Rapids, Michigan.

CHAPTER NINETEEN

BOB KREGEL ALSO WAS a remarkable man of God and man of faith. He was on a first name basis with some of the biggest names in Christianity. When I went into talk with Bob about teaching he graciously said, "Dave, I have always known that you are destined for ministry, but we don't want to lose you from being our Sales Manager so, why don't you do both next year." "Find out what classes they want you to teach and when they want you to teach them and still be our Sales Manager." I was totally dumbfounded. Not only was he supportive of me teaching, he still wanted me to be the Sales Manager. I remember thinking, "that decision not to take a radio job in Grand Rapids was one of the best decisions I ever made in my life." So in 1984, I was Sales Manager of Kregel Publications and a part-time faculty member of the Grand Rapids School of the Bible and Music.

During my final years at Kregel, I developed a good friendship with another Kregel whose name was Harold. Harold Kregel had been a missionary in Spain for many years

Harold J. Kregel, Founder of
Editorial Portavoz—the Spanish publication
division of Kregel Publications.

and moved to Grand Rapids to continue his Spanish publication ministry. We went to CBA (Christian Booksellers Association) together, we stayed together, we laughed together and we prayed together.

Harold is now with the Lord. But just before I left Kregel, I talked with him and Bob about the possibility of publishing the eight volume set of *Systematic Theology* by Lewis Sperry Chafer. We had learned that it was no longer going to be printed by Dallas Theological Seminary and my recommendation was that this would be a theology that Kregel should print. Harold knew the work well.

In my opinion, the eight volume set of *Systematic Theology* by Lewis Sperry Chafer is the best systematic theology that has ever been written. It is the one we were required to study in school. I have read and own almost every theology that has been published and I still believe this is the best ever written.

One of the last times I ever saw Harold on this earth he said, 'Have you seen we finally published Chafer?' Every time I am in a Christian bookstore anywhere and see that theology, my mind goes back to that very moment in my life.

CHAPTER TWENTY

ONE OF THE THINGS that was required for graduation was a written thesis. At the beginning of the graduation year, we had to submit in writing what we intended to research and it had to be approved as a thesis project.

I decided to write a thesis on the phrase "the husband of one wife"

Chris, Adam, Mary and myself taken during my days at Kregel and Grand Rapids School of the Bible.

which is found in the two New Testament books of 1 Timothy and Titus. For the most part, I had been in churches that said the phrase meant that one who had been divorced was disqualified from ministry and I had accepted that and decided to write a thesis supporting that view.

Two things happened at this time - early in my senior year - that began changing my perspective. When I submitted my thesis topic to John Miles for approval and told him what I intended to do, he said "you better take a serious look at those texts in the original and see what they do say and what they don't say."

The second thing that happened that made me think I could be wrong was something Warren Wiersbe wrote to me in a letter. Since I had a year to get this project done, I asked him about the phrase "husband of one wife" and he sent me a letter which basically said this and I'll paraphrase, "check out the testimony and life of C.I. Scofield." C.I. Scofield was famous for the Scofield Reference Bible, for a correspondence course to train pastors, he was founder of CAM missions, he was a Bible teacher who had been used all over the world - including the mentor of Lewis Sperry Chafer, and he pastored several churches, one of which still bears his name in Dallas Texas. C.I. Scofield had been divorced.

Since my major had been Greek, I began crawling deep into the Greek text and deep into church history and what I concluded was the phrase 'husband of one wife' meant a man who desires to be a leader in a church must be devoted to one woman. He must be a one woman man. Since Paul obviously knew the word "divorce" because he used it in 1 Corinthians 7, and since he was not the kind of shy Apostle to mince words, I concluded if he meant that a leader in God's church should not be divorced, he would have said that.

This became a key turning point in my thinking, because I was faced with a decision. Do I continue to accept the traditional views of a church or do I stand on what the text does or does not actually say.

I opted to stand on the Word of God and I have never looked back.

Harold Kregel read my finished thesis before I turned it in and he asked for a copy, which I gave him. He said that he traveled to Pennsylvania on business and went to a very large church on a Sunday morning and a pastor was speaking on this very passage. Harold said after the service, he went to the pastor and said I have something I would like you to read. I'll leave it with you and pick it up when I am back here again. The pastor agreed.

Months later Harold was back in that church and he said when the pastor spotted him, he came to Harold and said I want you to know that thesis has changed this church. God used it in a remarkable way in my life and in the life of this church. When Harold told me this story, I couldn't help but praise God for John Miles and for Warren Wiersbe, who knew things and saw things I didn't.

CHAPTER TWENTY ONE

AFTER GRADUATION, I had just a few months to prepare to teach part-time in the fall.

I was assigned two New Testament books to teach: Romans and Revelation.

When my brother Tim was in Dallas Seminary, my wife and I took a trip to visit him.

Adam and Chris at my graduation.

We were there over a weekend and naturally we wanted to attend church. Actually we ended up attending three services that Sunday at three different churches, but the one that stood out to me and ultimately would affect the way I prepare to preach and teach was a service at Believer's Chapel and the preacher was Dr. S. Lewis Johnson.

On the Sunday we went to his church, Dr. Johnson was expounding the Book of Genesis. As we walked into the vestibule of the church, an usher handed me a manuscript. I asked him what this was and he said "this is a copy of the exposition you are about to hear." All the way through school we were required to be involved in a local church and I was used to seeing some outlining and taking a few notes, but I had never seen anything quite like this.

As we took our seat, I thought, this ought to be interesting. I already have in my hands the message that is going to be preached. When Dr. Johnson started expounding the text, it was phenomenal. He spoke for nearly an hour and it seemed like five minutes. I followed along with his notes and frankly, I never wanted the study to stop.

But right there and then, I made a decision that if ever I were in a position to teach or preach in a church, I was going to be a manuscript preacher. It requires a great deal of preparation and honesty with a text to hand out a complete exposition like Dr. Johnson did, but that is what I purposed to do and I still do this to this very day.

While I was at Believer's Chapel I learned they had a tape ministry of various Bible book expositions and two of the books of the Bible that they had expounded were Romans and Revelation. Now their expositions of a Bible book were anything but shallow. They were exegetically thorough, grammatical, historical and theological. S. Lewis Johnson had done Romans and Bill McRae had done Revelation. I had already taken both of those books in school, but I decided to take advantage of their scholarship and listen to them. So that summer, I listened to their exposition, diagrammed and analyzed my Greek text, studied all solid commentaries I could get my hands on in preparation for my two courses.

As I prepared to teach that first semester, I divided the number of verses in a book by the number of hours for the class. This let me know exactly where I needed to be every class period. I prepared all my lectures in manuscript form and I still prepare and preach this way today.

One thing that always troubled me when I was in school or setting in a lecture series is that some professors rarely finished the book, which I never thought was right. I had paid money for a course to go through a book and then would get into a class and the teacher would wander and ramble and by the time the semester was over, we hadn't accomplished the goal. I always felt that was terribly wrong and I purposed never to teach like that.

One particular book that stands out in my mind was Proverbs. I truly wanted to go through the Book of Proverbs, and was excited about studying it, but by semester's end, the class knew more about the teacher than the book. I never wanted to be a teacher like that and when students finished any course I taught, my goal was that they understood the book in a way that God would deem "rightly divided."

God blessed that first year of teaching and I literally saw my classes fill up through the systematic teaching of God's Word. This would become a philosophy of ministry that has stuck with me all of these years.

CHAPTER TWENTY-TWO

DURING THAT YEAR IN 1984, I was both the Sales Manager for Kregel Publications and a part-time Bible teacher at the Grand Rapids School of the Bible and Music. When I traveled during that summer, I would take all of my books with me and my nights were spent preparing lectures. During the school year, I would make various sales trips to necessary locations to promote and sell Kregel Publications and then fly back in time to teach my classes.

One morning, that I distinctly remember, I pulled up to a red light at about 6AM and could not remember if I were headed to the airport or the school, so I knew sooner or later, I would need to make a decision to either stay at Kregel or go into ministry full-time.

By now, I had a very unique relationship with John Miles. He had been my teacher and mentor and now he was also my part-time boss. My first year of teaching had been well received and when I told him of my thoughts, in pure grace, he asked if I would consider joining the faculty full-time.

I was totally humbled and honored, but I also knew it would mean I would have to say goodbye to Kregel Publications and Bob Kregel.

CHAPTER TWENTY-THREE

I REMEMBER THE MEETING with Bob like it was yesterday. I'll never forget what he said and what he did. The truth is, God had blessed sales during that year and it was a privilege to be part of it.

When I went into his office, I told him that I had been asked to teach full-time at the Bible School and that I wanted to talk the matter over with him. Bob had been a wonderful boss to me and had taught me much about ministry and theological publications. He once told me, "Let me look at a pastor's library for 10 minutes and I'll tell you what kind of preacher he is." I have never forgotten that and I have discovered that this is absolutely true.

When I told Bob I felt I needed to leave and go to ministry full-time, here is basically what happened. First, he said, "Is there anything we could offer you to get you to stay?" I said no, they already were giving me plenty. Then he grinned and said, "I've always known this day would come because I've always known you were destined for ministry." He said, "When you leave there will be a bonus check waiting for you in appreciation of all you have done." The tears were rolling down my eyes and I said "Thank you very much. It has been an honor to know you and to work for you."

I don't know if Bob ever knew it, but we put that bonus check in the bank and when I would take my first pastorate, that bonus check would become part of the down payment on our first house.

CHAPTER TWENTY-FOUR

TEACHING AT THE Grand Rapids School of the Bible and Music was a great privilege, and a tremendous responsibility. Preparing men to serve God is no light task.

I was assigned to teach several courses from 1984-1986, including Public Speaking, Homiletics (both Junior and Senior level) which is the art and science of preparing and delivering Bible messages, Romans, 1 Corinthians and Revelation. When Mr. Miles was traveling, he would also have me substitute in his doctrine classes.

On most weekends, I would speak in different churches when their pastor was either on vacation, or the church was in between pastors.

I used my summer time to carefully prepare each course and each syllabus. As was my habit, I would break each class down by dividing the amount of material which was needed to be covered by the number of classes I had to work with and in this way knew exactly where I needed to be in every class.

I required that men in Senior Homiletics had to preach through one book of the Bible. Each man was required to preach a book in eight messages and I made them script out their entire expositions. I gave them fair warning in their Junior year that this would be their assignment and gave them all summer to get ahead in their work, if they so chose.

Here is the way my syllabus read: "Each student will preach eight expository messages that average 6-10 verses each. Six of the messages

Dr. John Walvoord, theologian, writer, teacher, and past-president of Dallas Theological Seminary.

will be 10-12 minutes in length and two of them will be 20 to 25 minutes. It is expected that you will dress for the occasion, maintaining a dignity for the pulpit ministry. You may preach through one of the following books: Galatians, Ephesians, Philippians, Colossians, 1 & 2 Thessalonians, 1 & 2 Timothy, Titus, 1 & 2 Peter, 1 John."

My goal in having them do this was that they learn the discipline of systematically expounding God's Word "line on line, precept upon precept." I am still of the conviction that God's power is unleashed when His Word is accurately expounded and to do this in a systematic way is tough work that demands much prayer and preparation.

I was at a gathering of ministers one time that featured Dr. John Walvoord who was undoubtedly one of the greatest, if not the greatest, student and teacher of biblical prophecy that God ever permitted to live on this earth. After Dr. Walvoord was introduced, he got up and said, "Men your ministries will be most effective not when a scholar leaves the service saying that was deep, but when a six year-old girl leaves the service and says I understood everything you said."

I never forgot that and I always communicated that to my students. I told them that to take God's infinite Word and expound it systematically and accurately so that it could be understood by a child is very demanding work that takes hours of preparation. Any one can stand up and verbally ramble, but to accurately expound a book requires intense work.

One dear man who came to my Homiletics class was already a pastor in a particular denomination. He was a good man who loved God, and he thought because he was already a pastor that he automatically knew how to preach. When it came time for him to preach his messages, he would read the text and then wander all over the place presenting one idea after another. The ideas weren't bad; they just were not true to the text. I would always grade him down and instruct him to handle what the text actually says. But time after time, he would stand up read his verses and then just start rambling about whatever he wanted to say.

Finally, in one of his messages, I gave him an "F." I don't know if I felt more sorry for him or for those to whom he preached in his church. One afternoon he knocked on my office door and he came in and said this: "My people in my church tell me that I have a way with words and yet when I come into your class, I can't seem to get a good grade. Why is that?"

My response was this—"You do have a wonderful way with words and you have a good way of saying those words, but now what we need to do is to get those words to line up with what that text actually says and you are not doing that. Your job is not to expound your political or social views about various topics; your job is to carefully and accurately 'preach the word.' (2 Timothy 4:1-2). God gave sixty-six inspired books to His people and your job is to give your people an accurate exposition of those books."

Those years at the Grand Rapids School of the Bible and Music were some of the best years of our lives. I developed a very close relationship with John Miles. He had been my teacher, my professor, my mentor, my model and now he was all of those things and two more: he was my boss and my friend. He was a very busy man with a demanding schedule, but he would always take time to talk with me and pray with and for me. It was during 1985, that he announced that he was going to retire and it was in 1986 that I would leave the school and take my first pastorate.

The Grand Rapids School of the Bible is no more. It ended up merging in later years with another college but as one teacher at both schools told me, "the education you received is no longer in existence."

When John Miles retired, the school started dwindling. I am totally convinced he was God's man for that institution. Just as there will never be another Martin Luther and his Reformation, so there will never be another John Miles and his school. He was the link to Dr. Chafer and the theological glue that held everything together and when he was gone, so was the school.

I just thank God that by His amazing sovereign grace, He let me share in the ministry of a man and his school that changed thousands of lives, including mine.

CHAPTER TWENTY-FIVE

WHILE I WAS IN SCHOOL working for Kregel, as already mentioned, Bob sent me to Cincinnati to make a 20 minute book presentation with five other publishers and one of the other publishers was Moody Press. The representative for Moody Press was a man named Dennis Getz and there was no way that anyone except God could know that five or six years later, he would play a key role in beginning my pastoral ministry.

I met Dennis on that first trip to Ohio, but after that he often traveled to Michigan to make sales calls on Christian bookstores and I would see him on occasion. Over time, we developed a friendship and often when Dennis was in Grand Rapids, he would come to our home and we would fellowship in the Lord and laugh about all kinds of things. He too had been saved by God's grace out of a worldly background. The thing that stands out in my mind about Dennis is that he had a deep love and reverence for the Word of God and he was drawn to people who had the same focus. He viewed his job at Moody as more than just a job. It became his ministry entrustment from God, which is exactly how a man's job should be viewed.

When I was promoted to Sales Manager for Kregel, we would often end up at the same Christian Bookseller events. Dennis knew of my love for Bible exposition and of the books I would have in my motel room in preparing for my teaching responsibilities at the Grand Rapids School of the Bible and Music. On one occasion, when his church in Indiana needed a guest speaker, he asked if I would be willing to fill the pulpit and I agreed. As I said, I preached almost every weekend in a different church and after my first trip to Indiana, I was often invited back to expound the Scriptures.

Dennis was an Elder in Community Bible Church in DeMotte, Indiana. DeMotte is a distant southeast suburb of Chicago. What I find so amazing, as I think back on all of this, is the timing of the sovereignty of God between John Miles and Dennis Getz. Just after Mr. Miles had announced he would be retiring, the pastor of the church in DeMotte resigned and because of a unique relationship that had been developed between two guys who worked for two different publishers, I was ultimately invited by the congregation to become pastor of the church.

It had been ten years since I had trusted Jesus Christ as Savior and now ten years later the summer of 1986, we packed up everything we owned to head west. I didn't know at the time but this move west would turn out to be 15 year journey. We said goodbye to Michigan, and we moved to our first church to become Pastor of Community Bible Church in DeMotte, Indiana.

CHAPTER TWENTY-SIX

WHEN I TRUSTED Jesus Christ I was 26 years old and at age 36, with
five years of education and three years of teaching behind me, I became Pastor of Community Bible Church in DeMotte, Indiana. What
God had done in nine plus years in our lives was truly "amazing
grace." DeMotte would become our home and our ministry for the
next seven years.

We had a wonderful ministry in DeMotte. The people were loving
and caring and they loved the Word of God. We saw people come

My first study in DeMotte at Community Bible Church.

to Christ and we saw people fall in love with the Scriptures. We had a fabulous youth group who would actually get up very early in the morning before school on Thursdays to come to a "Teen Breakfast" that my wife and others would make. They would come to church and I would teach them doctrine and we would pray and then we would get them to school.

The church grew all seven years and even on our last Sunday, we welcomed new members in to the church. I learned a lot about leadership and life. I learned how to confront things biblically. I had the great joy of marrying people and the grave heartache of burying people.

Frankly, there is nothing that can actually prepare you for your first pastorate. There are things you must and will face that you cannot and will not be able to learn from any college textbook. But I always found that no matter what the task, God was faithful. Daily, I would ask God to give me wisdom and ask Him to help me, and He always did.

The church grew under a philosophy of careful systematic exposition of God's Word.

I have never wavered from this philosophy because I truly believe it is exactly what God has prescribed in His Word. Growing a church through careful exposition of God's Word is not a flashy or quick way to get growth, but it is God's way to get it. It is like building a foundation on a rock and not sand. You can get something up much quicker if you build it on sand, but if you want to build something that will stand, it needs to be built on a rock and that is what biblical exposition does.

Pastoring a church is a demanding and daunting challenge. But I am totally convinced that no matter what the pressure, a minister must never allow anyone or anything to pull him away from careful, prayerful study of God's Word to feed God's flock. When a minister stays focused on this goal, God's sheep will come to eat a good meal. We saw all of our services increase in numbers, Sunday morning, Sunday evening and Wednesday. People came because they knew they would be fed. This was a great lesson I learned in DeMotte.

I was ordained in this church in 1992 and the key speaker at my ordination service was John Miles, who was then retired and pastoring a church in Michigan.

The ministry had been blessed by God and when I ended up believing it was God's will to leave, seven years later, it was truly a scene out of Acts 20:37. We were all literally weeping. I could not have asked for a better first church to pastor.

I had trusted Jesus Christ on June 10, 1976 and on June 21, 1992, over 16 years later, the elders of the church presented me with this letter (which will always hang in my office until the day God takes me home):

"We the Elders of Community Bible Church, having had the full and sufficient opportunity to examine and judge the quality and character of gifts and life of David E. Thompson herein, publicly testify and recognize the following:

That he has been gifted by God and called by God to the gospel ministry.

That his ministry has had a positive effect on God's people and the edification of His church.

That he has been an effective minister in evangelism, education and edification through his faithful service and godly character.

We, the undersigned, do commend and ordain for ministry David E. Thompson, this 21st day of June in the year of our God 1992."

Richard E. Anderson, Charles Kubal
Frederick Baxter, Leland R. Meiss
Dan Germann, Stanley T. Scholl

Dennis L. Getz, Paul Wierman
Wilmer Kooy

There are times when I look at this letter from our first church and fight back tears for the amazing grace of God. I did not deserve the privilege of being a pastor and I certainly did not deserve the privilege of unraveling Almighty God's precious written Word, but this is what God had done. This is what God called me to do.

You cannot earn a letter like this in any theological institution. There is only one way to get it. It comes from people whose lives have been changed by the power of God's Word. Above all other lessons I ever learned in DeMotte, the one that stands out the most is carefully feed God's people God's Word and His people will love it.

CHAPTER TWENTY-SEVEN

ONE SATURDAY AFTERNOON in the spring of 1992, I received a phone call from a man in Pocatello, Idaho and this is the essence of how the conversation went:

"Is this Pastor Thompson?"

"Yes it is."

"Pastor, I am an elder of Pocatello Bible Church and we are without a pastor and we are looking for a very serious, systematic Bible teacher and we understand that you are such a man."

"Yes, that is true, I am."

"Are you happy and content with your present ministry?"

"Yes"

"Are you looking to move?"

"No"

"Would you consider moving?"

"The only thing that would cause me to consider it would be if God moved in my mind and heart to consider it."

"We are looking for a man who does what you do and wonder if you would be willing to send us two to three consecutive Bible expositions so we may listen and compare them."

"Yes, I will send you that."

With that, I got the man's address, said goodbye, put the tapes in the mail and prayed and kept focused on my church ministry in DeMotte.

I have always had a close and open relationship with my elders and I met with them and told them exactly what happened and we prayed and that was that.

Several weeks went by and one day I received another phone call from Pocatello, Idaho. The essence of the phone call this time was that we would like to fly you and your wife out here to speak so we may determine what God's will is in this. I told them I would need to talk with my elders first to see what their opinion was.

When I met with the elders, they said 'we do not want you to leave this church, but we also always want you to do God's will, so we think you should fly there and see what God is doing in all of this.'

We flew to Pocatello, Idaho in the early summer of 1992 and a couple weeks later, we were voted in by the congregation and invited to become their pastor.

This put me in a real dilemma. I loved our church, our people and my board. Mary left the decision to me and we prayed. I spent two weeks in prayer seeking God's will and our elders were praying and ultimately it came down to this: "It is not that I had a sense that I must say yes to going to Pocatello, it is that I had a sense I could not say no."

I'm not sure how God's Spirit works with other men, but this is how it worked in my life. I had been approached by different churches from time to time to see if I would be interested in moving and there was no sense of urgency or prompting of God in any way. But in the Pocatello call, I just couldn't seem to shake it. I couldn't seem to say no to this congregation and it was that reality that led me to accept the call to go to Idaho.

Our final Sunday in DeMotte was June 28, 1992 and it was very emotional. It was hard on my wife, my children and me and it was hard on our people. All of us were weeping that final Sunday because God has truly blessed His Word in Community Bible Church and we had a true love and unity that had been produced by God's Spirit because of this.

One letter that shows what God had done was written by one of our teens whose name was Lisa Baxter and here is what she wrote: "Dear Pastor, I will miss you and Mary, Chris, and Adam very much. You have been a blessing to me spiritually. Mary is a sweetheart and dear friend. I know God is guiding you to Idaho to help that church grow spiritually and theologically. But I will miss you folks dearly. But I know you have to follow God. I will also miss you Mary, Chris and Adam. In God we Trust. Proverbs 3:5-6"

As we pulled out of DeMotte in July of 1992, we stopped at the church, prayed and cried. God had blessed us here and now nearly seven years later, we were again moving west.

CHAPTER TWENTY-EIGHT

To THIS POINT, OUR teaching ministry in Grand Rapids had been blessed by God and our first pastoral ministry in Indiana had been blessed by God and, as you will see, our pastoral ministry in Michigan has been amazingly blessed by God, but in between DeMotte and Kalamazoo was a bizarre eight year ministry in Pocatello that may have been blessed by God, but certainly not in any way like it was in DeMotte. God may have called me to Pocatello, but I'll have to wait until I'm in heaven until I'll know why.

I heard Dr. Chuck Swindoll once tell of a ministry that he had and he said the best thing about it was seeing it in his rearview mirror as he drove out of town, heading to another ministry. For me that kind of ministry was Pocatello, Idaho.

Pocatello was a grueling eight year ministry in which nothing I tried seemed to work.

Everything I believed God wanted me to do to build a strong church backfired. My intensity for God's Word didn't sit well or fit well in Pocatello.

A couple of blessings did come out of that ministry and one was I developed a true love for the Rocky Mountains and elk hunting. By foot and by horse, I saw God's creation in ways few will ever see it. On both the Idaho and Wyoming side of the Tetons, I learned places to hunt elk that not too many will ever know or will ever see. I used to love getting alone with God in those mountains. I have climbed up on top of some of the most unique mountains in the entire world and I have read the Word of God and prayed in places that truly do display the awesome majesty of God.

Another blessing of Idaho was the most straight shooting man I ever met, Larry Goetz. Larry was a straight shooter with any gun you put in his hands and he was a straight shooter with truth. He was so skilled at shooting guns that gun clubs used to get him to shoot when they were having bird/dog competitions and many would want him to sight in their rifles. He could sight in a rifle from scratch to hit dead center at one hundred yards in just six bullets.

When it came to being a man who stood for the truth of God's Word and God's work, no man was any more reliable than Larry. If he said it, you could count on it to be true. His father had once taught him, 'if a man's word is no good, the man is no good.' Larry never forgot that and he lived it. He did not exaggerate, but he would look you square in the eyes and tell you the truth. He loved our ministry and he loved God's Word and he remains a dear friend to this day.

One of the more dramatic stories of my entire ministry occurred in Pocatello.

One day there was a knock at my office door and when I opened the door there stood a lovely woman who said this, "I have heard you are a man who will tell me the truth and you are my last stop. If you cannot help me, I am going to kill myself." Talk about putting pressure on a pastor, the opening sentence this woman hit me with certainly raised the stakes of the meeting. I asked her to step into my office and asked her what seemed to be the problem.

She proceeded to unfold a sordid story of a life that had been filled with a lot of wrong choices and a lot of sin. When she got done, I said, "I have some good news for you. You can leave this office today totally clean and totally forgiven of everything you have ever done." I then proceeded to tell her about Jesus Christ and everything He did on the cross to save her. As I was sharing the gospel with her, the tears began to roll down her face and she said, "I need Jesus Christ in my life" and right where she sat, she invited Him into her life to be her Savior.

I told her that I wanted her to come to our church on Sunday, but she informed me that she was on her way to California. So I gave her a little basic doctrine book and I gave her my business card and told her that she needed to find a good church that teaches the Bible and if she ever had any questions, she could give me a call.

One Saturday morning about 2AM, my phone rang and it was her. She said, I am in a good church and I am going through this doctrinal book you gave me and I have some questions. I thought to myself, maybe it would be better to have this discussion at a different hour, but I praised God she called and answered her questions.

When I was at my office a couple years later, packing my books, getting ready to leave Idaho for a church in Michigan, there was a knock at my door. I opened the door and there stood a strange woman, whom I had never met before. She asked if I were Pastor Thompson and said "yes." She said, "Pastor, you do not know me, but you did know my sister." I said yes.

She said, my sister just died and I want you to know that her final couple of years on earth were spent serving the Lord and I know I will see her again. She grabbed my hand and said "thank you."

When she left, I started to cry. Maybe there was some good fruit that had been produced in Idaho.

I have been in full-time ministry now for well over twenty-five years and frankly I will never figure out what went wrong in the church in Idaho. What I do know is that when we were leaving, I was saying a hearty amen to the words of Dr. Swindoll.

CHAPTER TWENTY-NINE

JON CARR WAS THE chairman of the board of Texas Corners Bible Church in Kalamazoo, Michigan and Texas Corners Bible Church was without a pastor. Jon had grown under a ministry of systematic Bible exposition and he knew that the church needed a Bible expositor. At the time, I did not know Jon and Jon did not know me.

Jon had been speaking with a minister whom God had greatly used in his life, Doug Connelly, who was the pastor of a church in another part of the state. Jon expressed his desire for a Bible expositor and Doug mentioned my name.

I had always appreciated Doug's ministry. He was a very serious man of the Word and we had met years earlier at the Grand Rapids School of the Bible and Music and were of kindred mind because we both believed in systematic Bible exposition.

Jon Carr first called us in Idaho back in the fall of 1997 and asked if I would be willing to come and guest speak. It just so happened that I was planning to officiate at a marriage of a young lady in our former church in DeMotte in December and told him that I would be in the area. I agreed to guest speak and I did. The people were very receptive and we flew back to Pocatello thankful for the opportunity to preach God's Word.

Jon said that the church was just beginning to look for a minister but after I preached, he said "you became the benchmark" of what we wanted. So three months later, they called and asked if I would be willing to come and take a look at the church as a candidate, which I did in March of 1998.

One of the first questions that they asked me in meeting with the pulpit committee was whether or not I had read their constitution, and I answered "yes." The second question was if I agreed with their constitution and I answered "no." I explained that their constitution stated that the first purpose of church discipline was the restoration of the one under discipline and that the Bible teaches that the first purpose of church discipline is the purity of the church, which is clearly taught by Paul in I Corinthians 5:3-7. Jon would later tell me that further cemented that they thought I was God's man for this church.

Mary and I went back to Idaho and Texas Corners Bible Church voted to call us to come to be the Pastor. I prayed and wrestled with God on the matter for a couple of weeks and just could not seem to say "yes" at that time. I contacted Jon and told him.

Jon still believed I was God's man for the church so he called the church to pray for 30 days and he called me again. Again I wrestled and again I could not say "yes" at that time. I kept ministering in Idaho and Texas Corners Bible Church went on for their search for a minister.

Jon said for one year they looked at all kinds of ministers and all kinds of resumes, but they were not finding the Bible expositor they were looking for so one year later in the spring of 1999, they called us again in Idaho and invited us to become their pastor.

At this point I did sense God was stirring toward Kalamazoo so I went to God in prayer. I will admit that this was one time I was perplexed as to what to do and so I actually went to God and laid out a fleece, which is something I am not sure I would do today.

I had wrestled with God for nearly two weeks and could not decide. One of our sons had been looking for a job and I remember getting down on my knees and praying a prayer that went something like this. "God you know I want to do your will and it seems your will wants us in Kalamazoo, but I don't know, so if your will is for us to go to Michigan at this time do not allow our son to get a job, but if your will is for us to stay in Idaho then give him a job by 4:00PM on Friday, because at 4:00PM I will call Jon Carr and let him know one way or the other."

It seems to me, as I recall, that I began to pray that prayer very early in the morning and very early in the week. Every day when our son would come home he would inform us that he had not been able to find a job. Finally Friday came and nothing. It was 3:30PM on Friday afternoon and nothing. With 15 minutes to go, 3:45PM, our son walked into our home and said, "Dad I just got a job." I called Jon and told him that at that present time, I believed it was God's will to stay in Idaho.

Jon and the committed congregation were disappointed and they ultimately found another man to come as a pastor, but in August of 2000, he resigned.

CHAPTER THIRTY

IN AUGUST OF 2000 our church in Pocatello decided to have a family camp in the mountains. On Friday afternoon, we drove to a mountain range and put up tents and hauled in horses and supplies. Our plan was to have a campfire sing and prayer on Friday and Saturday night, and then have our main church service on Sunday morning, followed by a big potluck prepared by our ladies on Sunday and then pack up and go home.

Sunday morning a strange car drove back to where we were in the mountains. A man and his wife got out of the car and walked to where the people were gathering and asked if he could stay. We agreed. We had our service and after the service he asked if he could speak to me privately.

We walked out of the earshot of the people and he told me that he was on the board of a theological institution, whose president was stepping down. Years before I had done lectures at this school and he asked if I would be willing to pray about the possibility of becoming the next president of the school.

I was flabbergasted. Here we were deep in the Rocky Mountains and some stranger was asking me to pray about something I had not ever considered. I agreed to pray and went on with the weekend. We packed up our camp, loaded up the horses and drove back to Pocatello, Idaho and Mary and I prayed about what had happened that weekend.

Mary was in the house putting things away and I was outside unloading horses and camping equipment when she came out and said Jon Carr is on the phone from Texas Corners Bible Church.

I took the phone and Jon said our pastor is resigning and we are coming back to you again asking if you would consider becoming the pastor of Texas Corners Bible Church.

I agreed to very seriously consider it and he said he would get back with me.

I hung up the phone and said to Mary, it appears as if God is going to move us somewhere because what are the chances that two different ministries contact you to consider being their minister on the same day?

I immediately called my friend and mentor John Miles and he said to me, "you had better take a serious look at Kalamazoo because it is very rare that a church would go after a minister as that church has gone after you. It is very possible that God wants you in Kalamazoo at Texas Corners Bible Church."

So after much prayer and another trip to Texas Corners, we finally agreed in December of 2000 that it was God's will to come to Texas Corners Bible Church in Kalamazoo, Michigan and on the first Sunday in March of 2001, I stepped into the pulpit as the official Pastor.

CHAPTER THIRTY ONE

At the time we began the ministry there were about 40 people in the church and by God's amazing grace, as I write this, there are today between 400-500 people. God started blessing the ministry immediately.

Jon Carr had visited us in Idaho and both of us remember sitting in our home talking about the possibility of being back on the radio and teaching God's Word. One year after arriving in Kalamazoo, that became a reality.

The exterior of WKMI in 1976.

We decided to start a radio program called "Radio Bible Study" and purchase time on WKMI radio from 8-8:30 Sunday morning. We decided to teach straight through books of the Bible and never ask people for any money.

God has blessed this ministry and just recently a man wrote us to say that he remembered my voice from the 70's and has come to faith in Jesus Christ listening to the same voice on the same radio station 37 years later.

Mary and me in Kalamazoo shortly after becoming
Pastor of Texas Corners Bible Church.

The voice is familiar, but the message is different. God has brought us full circle.

We are on many radio stations all over the country and our free internet ministry is heard all over the world.

My story is simply the testimony of God's sovereign grace. He has transformed my life from a radio broadcaster to a Bible expositor.

If God can do that with me, He can do that with anyone. No matter what your past or sin, if you will turn your life to Jesus Christ, He will give you meaning, purpose, joy and fulfillment.

POSTSCRIPT

THE MINISTRY IN Texas Corners Bible Church has been and continues to be an amazing journey. We literally now hear from people all over the world. But this story is not just about me. The fact is, God has brought key people into the church, who have been greatly used by Him. It would be impossible to name them all but here are a few:

Jon Carr continues to be a powerful leader and board chairman in the church. It was his vision that brought this ministry to Kalamazoo.

John Breedveld was raised up by God to help develop and expand our radio ministry, taking it to an incredible level.

Ruth Koetje was raised up by God to become my first secretary with a love for this ministry that helped to build and promote the church all over the world.

Jim and Helene Lenfield were raised up by God to become our dear friends and strong defenders of a no nonsense approach to ministry with a passion for God's Word and doctrine.

Dennis, Sherry, Hollie Fritts who relocated from Idaho to Kalamazoo for a love of God's Word

Bob Windon, who was one of the first people saved in the sanctuary in our first exposition as pastor, is now a beloved Deacon and leader in the church.

Jerry Speedy was raised up by God to give incredible support and encouragement in many behind the scenes ways.

Mike Carr was raised up by God to start the Internet ministry

Michael Trumm was raised up by God to take the Internet ministry to a new world class level.

Tim Kelly was raised up by God to become a strong leader and defender of biblical exposition

Madelyn Goodrich, Deb Windon, Larry Boekeloo, Mary Louise Frederick, John Wolthuis, Beth

Koopsen were raised up by God to take our music to a powerful and reverent level.

Our board of Elders and Deacons who have all been led by God to carefully guard and protect all God has done and is doing in this church..

The entire congregation who continues to grow and mature as a body of believers, who truly do love God and His precious Word.

Texas Corners Bible Church and my life is still a work in progress. As A.T. Pierson used to say "History" is "His Story" and His story is a message of Amazing Grace and God's Amazing Grace will always be the story of my life.